Anonymous

Papers Relating to the State loan to the Boston, Hartford and Erie Railroad Company

1868

Anonymous

Papers Relating to the State loan to the Boston, Hartford and Erie Railroad Company
1868

ISBN/EAN: 9783744694308

Printed in Europe, USA, Canada, Australia, Japan

Cover: Foto ©ninafisch / pixelio.de

More available books at **www.hansebooks.com**

Commonwealth of Massachusetts.
Executive Department.
Boston,

PAPERS

RELATING TO THE

STATE LOAN

TO THE

BOSTON, HARTFORD AND ERIE

Railroad Company.

1 8 6 8.

BOSTON:

WRIGHT & POTTER, STATE PRINTERS,

No. 4 Spring Lane.

1868.

COMMUNICATION

OF

HIS EXCELLENCY GOVERNOR BULLOCK,

TO THE

HONORABLE COUNCIL.

COMMONWEALTH OF MASSACHUSETTS.

EXECUTIVE DEPARTMENT, BOSTON, }
October 14, 1868. }

To the Honorable Council:

The various matters which, by the act to aid the construction of the Boston, Hartford and Erie Railroad, chapter 284 of the acts of 1867, must be made to appear to the satisfaction of the Governor and Council before the issue of any scrip, are recapitulated in the report of the Committee of the Council.

Certain of these matters are required by the act to be made to appear to the satisfaction of the Governor and Council and the Attorney General; and certain others to the satisfaction of the Governor and Council and the Commissioners appointed under the sixth section of the act.

On the 31st of July, the Commissioners made an extended report upon the whole subject, and in conclusion expressed the opinion that, if the means and resources of the company should be honestly and judiciously used, and with a reasonable degree of energy, enterprise and economy, the road might be thereby constructed and moderately equipped, and they accordingly recommended the allowance, by the Governor and Council, of a loan of scrip for the work already done and equipment purchased. This report has been before the committee of the Council, and, with the documents which accompany it, is herewith submitted, marked A.

These documents were transmitted to the Attorney General, with the request that he would report upon the various matters in which his concurrent action was required. His reply has been before the Committee of the Council, and is herewith submitted, marked B.

It was quite obvious to my mind that it was the design of the legislature to secure the separate and responsible judgment of the Governor and Council upon each of the particulars named in the act as necessary to be shown. It also became early apparent that the principal questions concerning which doubts would exist, were, whether the requirements of the statute concerning the payment and cancellation of the mortgage debts secured by the underlying mortgages on that part of the road situate this side of Southbridge and Willimantic were complied with, and whether the company has satisfactorily shown that they would be able, without further aid from this Commonwealth, to complete their line from Boston to Fishkill before May 27, 1872.

Deeply impressed with the responsibility imposed upon me in respect to these questions, I have given my careful and personal attention to the examination of the details which could throw light upon them.

The attention of the Committee of the Council was called to the considerable discrepancy which was found to exist in the various statements of the bonds now outstanding, which are secured by the underlying mortgages above referred to. This discrepancy has been largely relieved by subsequent explanations ; and the recommendation of the Committee of the Council, that a bond with personal sureties should be required, in the penal sum of one million of dollars, to protect the franchise and property described in the Berdell mortgage from the uncancelled bonds, obviates the objections intimated in this report of the Attorney General, and dispenses with the necessity of a precise ascertainment of the number of bonds now outstanding, which indeed appears impracticable.

The Committee of the Council also became satisfied that the company will be able to complete their line of road to Fishkill within the time specified by the act, without further aid from this Commonwealth, as appears by their report, which is herewith submitted, marked C.

Wishing, however, rigidly to test the conclusion to which the Committee of the Council had come upon this latter subject, I addressed to the Commissioners a supplementary communication, which expressed the doubts that still remained in my mind, and the want of full information, which, as it seemed to me, still existed upon certain facts bearing upon the question; and this communication, with the reply of the Commissioners, is also submitted herewith, marked D.

By this reply, the validity of the acceptances of the Erie Railroad did not appear to be established, and I was not able quite to concur with the opinion of the Commissioners that it would seem a fair estimate to offset the accruing interest money, which the company would apparently be obliged to pay, against the earnings of the road. Up to this time it had been assumed that the full time allowed by the Act for the completion of the road to Fishkill might be occupied in doing the work. It was obvious that an amount of about $3,000,000 would become due for interest before that time. By the last exhibit of the Commissioners, the sums to be paid by the company exceeded their pecuniary resources, now within their control. There were also certain other matters of detail concerning which I desired further information. I therefore presented certain inquiries to the officers of the company, which, with their replies thereto, and an accompanying opinion of Mr. Evarts, are herewith submitted to you, marked E.

By these replies, it appeared that it is the purpose of the company to complete their line of road to Fishkill during the next year; and, upon personal conference with Mr. Ashburner, one of the Commissioners, and himself a civil engineer of large experience in this kind of work, I am satisfied that this may be done. This early completion of the road will greatly diminish the amount of interest to be paid.

This opinion of Mr. Evarts was submitted to the Attorney General, and he deems it satisfactory to establish the liability of the Erie Railroad Company for the bonds which they have received, as appears by his letter hereto appended, and marked

F. To this is added another communication, from the Attorney General, marked G.

. Upon the whole case, as thus presented, the question then remains, what rule is to be adopted as a guide by which to determine whether the company will be able to complete their line of road to Fishkill, without further aid from the Commonwealth? Are they to be required to demonstrate mathematically an actual present ability, from means now within their control, to meet the necessary disbursements? Or, do they meet the requirement of the statute by making it appear to the satisfaction of the reason and conscience that in all human probability they will be able to accomplish the work? Accepting the latter as the true rule, bearing in mind the valuation which the public have now for several months continuously put upon the shares of the company, and believing that this indicates the existence of a borrowing capacity on the part of the company yet remaining, which is equal to the difference between the required disbursements and their present actual means, I am prepared to submit for you decision the subjoined order.

I have given to the subject long and patient investigation, an amount of time, care and thought by no means represented by the brief terms in which I have here stated my conclusion. I believe the documents hereto appended will sustain the result I have reached; and I have confidence that the progress and completion of this road, and its future working operations, will confirm my opinion of its importance in the commercial relations of the Commonwealth.

ALEXANDER H. BULLOCK.

Ordered, That upon the due cancellation of the bonds taken up by the Boston, Hartford and Erie Railroad Company, which were secured by the underlying mortgages referred to in chapter 284, section 2, of the acts of 1867, or the stamping of them in a form and manner to be approved by the Governor, so as effectually to prevent their being negotiated hereafter,—such cancellation or stamping to be done under the direction of the commissioners,—and upon the execution of a bond with personal sureties to the satisfaction of the Governor and Council in the penal sum of $1,000,000, with condition as provided in the same section above referred to, and upon the execution of the agreement mentioned in section 3 of the same statute, and the delivery of the Berdell mortgage bonds therein provided for, scrip of the Commonwealth shall be issued and delivered to the treasurer of that company to the amount of $100,000, to be expressed in the currency of Great Britain.

[A.]

To His Excellency Governor Bullock *and the Honorable Council:*

The undersigned, having been appointed in pursuance of the Act of the General Court of May 27, 1867, among other things, "to advise and inform the Governor and Council in reference to all matters and things they are called upon to ascertain and verify under the terms and provisions of this Act," respectfully report that they have endeavored to ascertain the history and present condition of the various railroad corporations or roads which form constituent parts of the present corporation and road of the Boston, Hartford and Erie Railroad Company.

They have had in view, also, the ulterior consideration, how far the Governor and Council and Commissioners should be satisfied that said railroad company will be able to complete a line of railway from Boston to Fishkill, and that the same will be completed within five (5) years from the passage of said Act.

In making their investigations, the Commissioners have been aided in all things by the officers of the company, who have answered all inquiries and exhibited all documents and papers which the Commissioners have called for, without hesitation or apparent reserve.

The various steps and measures which the Commissioners have taken to arrive at their results, they are induced to state, somewhat in detail, that the Governor and Council may be able the more readily to judge how far the conclusions to which the Commissioners have come are well founded.

The Boston, Hartford and Erie Railroad, if completed as contemplated in said Act, will extend from tide-water in Boston by Blackstone, Willimantic, Hartford and Waterbury to Fishkill, and from Providence by Plainfield to Willimantic, with a branch from Blackstone to Southbridge. A plan, which accompanies this Report, will furnish an outline of these united lines between Providence and Fishkill, and Boston and Fishkill, with the branch to Southbridge. The plan will also show a line of chartered road, not yet begun, from Willimantic to New Haven, and one from Woonsocket to Putnam, upon which considerable work has been done, charters for which are held by the Boston, Hartford and Erie Company.

A reference to this plan will also serve to explain the various Acts of incorporation, which it becomes necessary to refer to in this connection, in order to trace the history of the present corporation.

Beginning with the part of the road which lies in Massachusetts, the first Act seems to have been, incorporating Walpole Railroad from the Dedham Branch to Walpole, in 1846, (c. 231.) In 1847; (c. 252,) Norfolk County Railroad was incorporated from Walpole to Blackstone, and the Walpole Railroad authorized to unite with it, and, as the papers show, this was done. In 1849, (c. 194,) Southbridge and Blackstone Railroad, from Blackstone to Southbridge, was incorporated.

In 1850, (c. 268,) the Midland Railroad was incorporated from the terminus of the Norfolk County Road to Boston, and this was authorized to unite with the Norfolk County and Southbridge Roads, which union appears to have been accomplished in 1853 under the name of the " Boston and New York Central Railroad."

In 1858, (c. 60,) this united road took a new name under a new incorporation, viz.: " Midland Railroad Company."

In 1861, (c. 155,) the "Midland Land Damage Company " was incorporated to assume the property, &c., of the Midland Railroad Company, which appears to have been done. And in 1863, (c. 116,) this corporation was changed to that of " South Midland Railroad Company," and this corporation was united with the Boston, Hartford and Erie road in 1863, as appears by their deed on record, which is referred to in the Act of 1865, (c. 275.)

One other line of railroad in this State, which forms a part of what is embraced under the charter of the Boston, Hartford and Erie road, consists of the " Charles River Branch Railroad," incorporated in 1849, (c. 170,) from Boston and Worcester Railroad in Brookline to Dover, and this was authorized to unite with the Charles River Railroad by an Act of 1851, (c. 297,) extending to Bellingham, under the name of the " Charles River Railroad." In 1855, this road was authorized (c. 105,) to extend its line to the line of Rhode Island, and to unite with a road incorporated in Rhode Island, called the New

2

York and Boston Railroad, and the union of these was con
firmed by Act of 1856, (c. 238.)

Passing now to the parts of said road situate in Rhode Island,
and chartered under the Acts of that State, the legislature, in
1846, incorporated a railroad called the "Providence and Plainfield Railroad," extending from Providence to Connecticut line,
and in 1852 confirmed the union between that and the Hartford, Providence and Fishkill Railroad, chartered in Connecticut. The Hartford, Providence and Fishkill road was subse-
quently united with the Boston, Hartford and Erie road in
Connecticut, and this union was confirmed by Act of Rhode
Island in 1865.

In 1866, the legislature of Rhode Island authorized the Boston, Hartford and Erie Railroad to locate and construct the
railroad which had been granted to the Woonsocket Railroad
Company to Pascoag and the line of Connecticut.

In 1858, the legislature of Rhode Island confirmed what is
called a union and merger of the Woonsocket Union Railroad
with the New York and Boston Railroad in Connecticut, and
recognized the union of these with the Charles River Railroad
in Massachusetts, forming thereby one company, under the
name of the "New York and Boston Railroad Company."

The history of the parts of this railroad which are within the
State of Connecticut appears to be as follows:

In 1833, the "Manchester Railroad" was incorporated. In
1847, its charter was renewed under the name of "Hartford
and Providence Railroad," and to extend its road to Willimantic, and in 1848 it was authorized to extend its road to the
eastern line of the State of Connecticut.

In 1845, the New York and Hartford Railroad, from Hartford
to the west line of the State, was incorporated, and in 1849
was united with the Hartford and Providence Railroad, under
the name of "Hartford, Providence and Fishkill Railroad;"
this union was confirmed by Act of 1852.

In 1846, the "New York and Boston Railroad" was incorporated from New Haven through Middletown to the east line of
the State, and in 1849 it was authorized to connect and unite
with other roads. Upon the accompanying map, this road is
laid down from New Haven to Willimantic, but a part only of
it has yet been wrought. In 1864, the legislature of Connecti-

cut extended the time of completing it, and renewed its charter. In 1857, "Thompson and Willimantic Railroad" was incorporated, uniting the lines or tracks of the Boston and New York Central with the New York and Boston Railroad. This is indicated upon the accompanying map as beginning at Willimantic and extending through Putnam to meet the extended line of road from Boston to Blackstone.

In 1863, the Boston, Hartford and Erie Railroad was incorporated by the legislature of Connecticut, and was organized July, 1863. In July, 1863, the corporation purchased and acquired the property, franchise, &c., of the Hartford, Providence and Fishkill Railroad. This was ratified by Rhode Island in 1865.

In September, 1863, the Southern Midland Railroad Company conveyed its franchise and property to the Boston, Hartford and Erie Railroad; in the same month, the same thing was done by the Thompson and Willimantic Railroad.

In December, 1864, the Boston, Hartford and Erie Railroad was united with the New York and Boston Railroad, and was authorized by an Act of the legislature of Connecticut to extend its road from Putnam to the line of Rhode Island.

In 1864, by an Act of the legislature of New York, the Boston, Hartford and Erie Railroad was authorized to unite with and purchase the "Boston, Hartford and Erie Extension Railroad," and the "Boston, Hartford and Erie Ferry Extension" franchises, those being corporations created in the State of New York, and a purchase was accordingly made by the Boston, Hartford and Erie Railroad of the franchise, &c., of the Boston, Hartford and Erie Extension Railroad in June, 1864.

By the action of the legislature of Massachusetts, during its last session, the Boston, Hartford and Erie road was established as a corporation in Massachusetts, as by reference to the Acts of the general court will appear.

The legislative Acts, as well as the deeds and contracts, and the corporate proceedings of those various corporations by means of which they have become merged or united in the existing corporation of the Boston, Hartford and Erie Railroad Company, have been found to be very numerous, not a little complicated, and such as to require much patient research and examination. But the result to which the Commissioners have come, upon a review of all these is, that the Boston, Hartford and Erie Railroad Corporation have a charter and franchise for a railroad from Boston to the North River, as indicated upon the map, by the way of. Blackstone, Putnam, Willimantic, Hartford and Waterbury to Fishkill ; also from Boston to New Haven by the way of Brookline, Woonsocket, Putnam, Willimantic and Middletown, some portions of both which lines are over and along the same route or location. And that the same corporation have also by their charter or franchise a railroad from Providence by the way of Plainfield to Hartford, and a railroad from Blackstone to Southbridge, all under one ownership, management and control.

The following schedule will show the lengths and distances of these various parts and portions of the railroad existing and contemplated belonging to said corporation, and what parts and portions of those are now in operation, and what are constructed or in process of construction, but not in use, and upon what parts or portions no work has yet been done, which is here furnished to enable the Governor and Council to judge somewhat of the condition and prospective capacities of the road, should it be completed :—

Memorandum of Distances, Boston, Hartford and Erie Railroad.

From Boston to Mechanicsville, built, . .	59.57 miles.
From Mechanicsville to Willimantic, building, .	26.28 "
From Willimantic to Waterbury, in operation, .	63.86 "
From Waterbury to Fishkill, under contract, with some little work partially begun, . . .	76.39 "
Total, ...	226.1 "

The above constitutes the proposed through line from Boston to Fishkill, and from this contemplated through line, there are to be the following branches :—

One from a point twelve miles from Boston, to Dedham, (incomplete), two miles.

One from North Wrentham, twenty-three miles from Boston, to Medway, (incomplete), four and five-tenths miles.

One from East Thompson, fifty-two miles from Boston, to Southbridge, (in operation), seventeen and five-tenths miles.

The line from Boston to East Thompson, and the branch to Southbridge, are at present in operation as a through line.

There is also a line in operation from Providence to Willimantic, (fifty-eight and one-half miles,) forming, with the line from Willimantic to Waterbury, the through line from Providence to Waterbury, called the Hartford, Providence and Fishkill Railroad, and not yet actually in possession of the Boston, Hartford and Erie Railroad Company.

And finally, there is the line in operation from Brookline to Woonsocket, thirty-three and three-fourths miles in length.

In going through with the investigations above referred to, the Commissioners became advised that there was an indebtedness in various forms outstanding against some or all of these various corporations, and they early took measures to ascertain what claims were thus outstanding, not so much with a view of passing upon the amount and justice of individual claims, as of approximating somewhat the financial condition of the present corporation. To this end, they caused advertisements to be published in one or more newspapers in New York, New Haven, Hartford, Providence and Boston, requesting such as had claims against any of those roads, which were not secured by mortgages upon their franchises, &c., to state their amounts to the Commissioners. In compliance with this request, claims of various kinds and amounts have been forwarded to the Commissioners, amounting in all to $69,380, besides sundry indefinite claims for land, of which, however, the officers of the corporation admit only a sum less in amount than $5,000 to be due, and denying the liability of the company beyond that sum, and will, as they say they believe, successfully contest the same, if prosecuted. This does not include a claim made for certain alleged preferred stock in the Hartford, Providence and Fishkill Railroad, which is contested by the Boston, Hartford and Erie Company, and their liability thereon is denied.

The measures adopted by the Commissioners to ascertain the amount for which any part of the road or its franchise was liable, which was secured by mortgage or mortgages upon the same, were these: They obtained from a well known and responsible counsellor at law in each of the States of New York, Connecticut and Rhode Island, certificates of the forms and places required by law for the recording of railroad mortgages in the respective States, and having done so, they obtained from the respective officers in these States and in Massachusetts, certified statements of what mortgages have been issued by the said corporations, which had been recorded therein. Having obtained these, the Commissioners, under the authority given them by the Act of the general court of the last winter, empowering them to take the testimony of witnesses in the prosecution of their inquiries, issued formal interrogatories, a form of which is hereunto annexed, addressed to one or more of the trustees, who were supposed to hold and have knowledge of any of the mortgages mentioned in any of said certificates. By the sworn answers to these interrogatories, they ascertained that the Boston and New York Central Railroad Company issued upon one mortgage bonds to the amount of $794,000 00

And the South Midland Railroad Company, upon another mortgage, ... 301,000 00

That the New York and Boston Railroad Company had issued upon one mortgage, . . 345,600 00

And upon another mortgage, ... 1,287,700 00

The witness stated that bonds of the Charles River Branch Railroad Company should be added, of the sum of 37,000 00

One of the trustees of the Norfolk County Railroad mortgage stated that in an investigation made by the Supreme Judicial Court, it was found that the amount of bonds then outstanding was 414,350 00

The Hartford, Providence and Fishkill Railroad issued upon mortgage, bonds to the amount of 2,055,000 00

To this is to be added arrears of interest, . . 170,000 00

And the Boston, Hartford and Erie Railroad, upon a mortgage made to the Treasurer of Connecticut, issued bonds to the amount of . 4,500,000 00

These make an aggregate of $9,904,650 00

This is independent of bonds issued by the Boston, Hartford and Erie Railroad Company, upon a mortgage of their entire road and franchise to Berdell and others. This forms so important a part of the means and resources of the road, that its character and condition should be more fully explained. The mortgage bears date of March 19th, 1866, and is conditioned to pay $20,000,000 in bonds, payable in the year 1900, with semi-annual interest at seven per cent. in New York or London, as the directors should authorize, and in the recital of the mortgage, these bonds are said to be issued for the purpose of providing for and retiring all existing mortgage debts and prior liens upon the line of the road, and for the purpose of completing and equipping their road, and of laying down a third rail, so as to form an additional track corresponding with the gauge of the Erie Railway of New York. A copy of this mortgage forms a part of this Report.

The legislature of Connecticut ratified and confirmed the making of this mortgage to Berdell and others in May, 1866. Rhode Island ratified the making of this mortgage, January, 1866, and New York, in April, 1866.

The legislature of Massachusetts, in 1865, (c. 275) authorized the Boston, Hartford and Erie Railroad Company to secure any bonds it had or might issue, by a mortgage upon its railway, franchise, &c., situated in Massachusetts, and in 1866, (c. 142) confirmed the doings of the company in the making of the mortgage to Berdell and others, with a view, as said Act · will show, of these bonds being substituted, as far as necessary, for the bonds then outstanding against the prior companies which had held the parts of the road within the State of Massachusetts.

The Act of 1867, (c. 284) under which these Commissioners were appointed, required that before any scrip should be loaned to the company, all underlying mortgages upon that part of the Boston, Hartford and Erie Railroad lying between the foot · of Summer Street, in the city of Boston, and the town of Southbridge, in Massachusetts, and Willimantic, in Connecticut, should be cancelled and discharged to less than one million of dollars, and a bond given conditioned that the parts of said railway above mentioned should be protected from all such uncancelled bonds.

The attention of the Commissioners was consequently called to the question how far this requirement had been complied with by the company, and also what amount of indebtedness of said company, in bonds or otherwise, was now outstanding. By the affidavit of the Hon. J. C. Bancroft Davis, one of the trustees in the Berdell mortgage, it appears that there had been, on June 4th, 1868, thirteen thousand bonds, of one thousand dollars each, signed by said trustees, nine thousand three hundred and thirty-seven of which had been delivered to the Boston, Hartford and Erie Railroad Company.

The depositions of more than one of the trustees in the earlier bonds tended to show that a very considerable part of those had been surrendered to the Boston, Hartford and Erie Company. Thus, J. W. Clark states that only $45,000 of those issued by the Boston and New York Central are outstanding, the balance being now in the possession of the Boston, Hartford and Erie Railroad Company, and that the entire amount issued by the South Midland Railroad Company are in the possession of the Boston, Hartford and Erie Company.

Mr. J. W. Converse, a trustee of the Norfolk County Railroad mortgage, states that nearly all the bonds issued upon that mortgage, and all of which he had obtained any information, are in the hands of the trustees, ready to be delivered to the Boston, Hartford and Erie road, under a satisfactory arrangement.

Mr. H. N. Farwell states that all the bonds issued by the New York and Boston Railroad, and by the Charles River Railroad, except $65,200, are in the possession of the Boston, Hartford and Erie road; and by a statement of the treasurer of the Boston, Hartford and Erie road, which is hereto annexed, it appears that the amount of said bonds which had been taken up before the date of the Berdell mortgage was $1,150,800, and since that, $5,963,000, leaving, of the above sum of $9,904,650 outstanding, $2,790,800, which includes also an item of interest outstanding of $170,000. Of this amount, the bonds of the Providence, Hartford and Fishkill Railroad constitute $2,055,000, on which the above item of interest is due. So that a sum clearly less than $1,000,000 remains outstanding upon any part of the road between Boston and Willimantic or Southbridge.

To ascertain what amount of said bonds had been taken up, and were in possession of the Boston, Hartford and Erie road,

Commonwealth of Massachusetts.

Executive Department.

William Dehon, Esq., was requested to count and examine them, and his report of such examination is herewith returned, showing that the aggregate, as counted by him, was $6,672,650, including an item of interest notes of $277,000, viz. : —

"To the Hon. GEORGE T. BIGELOW :

"I hereby certify that I have personally examined and counted sundry bonds and mortgage notes exhibited to me by the treasurer of the Boston, Hartford and Erie Railroad Company, as follows, viz. :

"South Midland Railroad Company bonds amounting to three hundred and one thousand dollars, ...	$301,000 00
"Norfolk County Railroad Company bonds amounting to four hundred and ten thousand seven hundred and fifty dollars, . .	410,750 00
"Boston and New York Central Railroad Company bonds amounting to seven hundred and sixty thousand dollars, ...	760,000 00
"New York and Boston Railroad Company bonds amounting to eight hundred and eighty-five thousand nine hundred dollars, .	885,900 00
"Charles River Railroad Company bonds amounting to sixteen thousand dollars, .	16,000 00
"Boston, Hartford and Erie Railroad Company bonds amounting to four millions and twenty-two thousand dollars, . . .	4,022,000 00
"New York and Boston Railroad Company mortgage notes amounting to two hundred and seventy-seven thousand dollars, . .	277,000 00
"Making in the aggregate, in bonds and notes, the sum of six millions six hundred and seventy-two thousand six hundred and fifty dollars, ...	$6,672,650 00

"BOSTON, July 25, 1868."

In either mode of computation, therefore, there appears to be considerably less than $1,000,000 outstanding upon that part of the road mentioned in the Act under which this Commission was created; so that, in that respect, the Boston, Hartford and Erie Railroad appear to have complied with the preliminary conditions upon which a loan of scrip was to be made by the Commonwealth.

In respect to the other subjects upon which the Commissioners were, by said Act, expected to report, one of them was, how far, in their judgment, the Boston, Hartford and Erie Railroad had within their command the means of completing a line of railway from Boston to the North River at Fishkill?

The treasurer states the present floating debt of the company to be $1,022,988.31, and the interest notes given upon exchange of the mortgage bonds, $1,127,744.14. The old issue of bonds outstanding, including interest in arrears, $2,790,800. And to these are to be added the amount of the Berdell mortgage bonds, sold or exchanged, and therefore outstanding against the company, of $10,963,000, making an aggregate, independent of anything due upon the first class of claims mentioned in this Report, of $15,904,532.45.

Of the assets or means at the command of the company, they hold, as stated by the treasurer, of the Berdell bonds not yet negotiated, the sum of $9,037,000, fifty thousand shares of capital stock not yet disposed of, cash on hand on deposit in bank, as certified by the cashier, $2,000,000, and acceptances of the Erie Railroad for $1,574,000.

The above may be regarded as convertible means at the market prices of the bonds and stock of the company.

The company has its road and its rolling stock, including the Hartford, Providence and Fishkill Railroad, above its mortgages, which, in the judgment of the Commissioners, may be fairly estimated at the sum of at least twelve million dollars, having reference to the present cost of such a road and equipment.

But as these are not a present means of raising money, they are not taken into account in judging of the capacity of the company to complete the road.

The company having reduced the mortgage upon the part of the road mentioned in the Act to less than $1,000,000, propose to deposit with the Commonwealth, at once, the full amount in the Berdell mortgage bonds of $4,000,000, to which the State by the Act would be ultimately entitled upon loaning its scrip to the contemplated amount of $3,000,000.

Of the importance of the road, if completed, to the business of Boston and the State, it is no part of the duty of the Commissioners to speak, except as it bears upon the probability of its being ultimately constructed and put in use. This undoubtedly entered into the consideration of the legislature in providing for a contingent loan of scrip. A glance at the map of New England and New York must satisfy any one that a road extending from Boston, through the region traversed by this road, and connecting directly with one of the great lines from the West, could not, when once built, fail to be the avenue of an immense and constantly increasing trade and business. The Commissioners have no better means of forming a judgment upon this point, however, than the Governor and Council, nor can it be a present convertible means out of which the road can be constructed, though it may be an element of credit upon which the road may hereafter raise an additional loan, if it becomes necessary.

In forming a judgment of the degree of confidence with which the Governor and Council may count upon the completion of the road by the present company within the time prescribed by the Act, reference must be had, in no small measure, to the character of its management, in judgment, fidelity and energy, and skill on the part of its officers and managers.

While the Commissioners have not gone into detail in respect to its present management, they have become satisfied that the enterprise is being carried forward with energy and a confident determination on the part of the president and directors; and that, if these are not suffered to be relaxed, the road may be completed within the time prescribed by the Act; and should there be cause hereafter to apprehend a failure to comply with the requirement of the Act, it will be competent for the Governor and Council, by the terms of the Act, at any time to withhold further advances of the loan.

The treasurer states that the present gross earnings of the road amount to the annual sum of $388,639.07, and that the value of the bonds and stock of the road is rising in the market as the work progresses.

The Commissioners have made the best estimate in their power of the probable cost of the road, as it has been projected, located and contracted for, including a moderate outlay for first equipment, which, for obvious reasons, it might not be policy to disclose in a public report, as they have meant to estimate it sufficiently high to meet the contingencies, and if published it might embarrass the company in making their contracts.

They, however, have compared this estimate with the means and resources of the company, as exhibited above, and they have come to the conclusion that, if honestly and judiciously used, and with a reasonable degree of energy, enterprise and economy, the road may be thereby constructed and moderably equipped.

In conclusion, the Commissioners respectfully report that they are satisfied :—*First*, That the Boston, Hartford and Erie Railroad Company have a good title to the franchise and railroad as described above, between Boston and Fishkill and Providence and Fishkill. *Second*, That the company have removed all underlying mortgage debt prior to the Berdell mortgage, upon that part of the road lying between Boston and Williamantic and Southbridge, except a sum less than $1,000,-000, now outstanding thereon. *Third*, That the company have the means, if aided by a loan of the scrip of the State, as proposed, and if prudently and properly used and managed, by which to complete the road to Fishkill and provide a moderate equipment therefor ; and *Fourth*, That if prosecuted with reasonable energy and good faith, the company may complete said road within the time prescribed in the Act providing for said Commission.

The Commissioners herewith make a recommendation for an allowance by the Governor and Council of a loan of scrip to the Boston, Hartford and Erie, for work already done and equipment purchased.

All which is respectfully submitted.

G. T. BIGELOW,
EMORY WASHBURN,
S. ASHBURNER,
Commissioners.

BOSTON, July 31, 1868.

*Condition of Bonded Indebtedness under the Mortgage to Robert H.
Berdell and Others, of date of March 16, 1866, for $20,000,000.*

Amount of bonds exchanged for bonds issued
by Boston and New York Central Railroad
Company; Norfolk County; Southern Midland; Charles River Branch; New York and
Boston; Boston, Hartford and Erie, March 1, ·
1864; New York and Boston mortgage notes, $5,963,000 00
Sold in New York, ... 5,000,000 00

                        $10,963,000 00

Owned by corporation, and held to take up all
underlying bonds, and for general uses of
Company, ... $9,037,000 00
Floating debt, July 20, 1868, ... 1,022,988 31
Amount of notes given for overdue interest on
exchanged bonds, and due Sept. 1, 1872, with
interest after Jan. 1, 1870, ... 1,127,744 14

H. S. BARRY, *Asst. Treas.*

I hereby certify that this covers the whole outstanding debts and liabilities
on account of existing contracts.   II. S. BARRY, *Asst. Treas.*

SUFFOLK, ss. July 30, 1868. Subscribed and sworn to as true before me,
          ·   ·   · G. T. BIGELOW, *Commissioner, &c., &c.*

Statement concerning Bonded Indebtedness on Franchise and Estate of Boston, Hartford & Erie Railroad Company.

Amount of bonds exchanged since mortgage
to Berdell and others, ... $5,963,000 00
Amount taken up before then, . . . 1,150,800 00
                                                           ──────────────
                                                           $7,113,800 00
Present bonded debt outside of Berdell mort-
gage,—
Hartford, Providence and Fishkill, . $2,055,000
Boston and New York Central, . 34,000
Boston, Hartford and Erie, mortgage
of 1864, ... 477,000
New York and Boston, . . . 54,800
Amount of int'st on Hartford, Prov-
idence and Fishkill bonds, . . 170,000
                                                 ──────── 2,790,800 00
                                                           ──────────────
                                                           $9,904,600 00

Amount of indebtedness at issue of Berdell and
other mortgages before then, . . . $9,904,600 00
Amount of bonded indebtedness resting on the
franchise and property between foot of Summer Street, Boston, and Southbridge in Mass.
and Willimantic in Conn., ... 511,000 00

H. S. BARRY, *Asst. Treas.*
BOSTON, July 25, 1868.

SUFFOLK, ss. July 30, 1868. Subscribed and sworn to as true before me,
G. T. BIGELOW, *Commissioner.*

To His Excellency the Governor and the Honorable Council of the Commonwealth of Massachusetts:

The undersigned, Commissioners appointed under an Act of the legislature of said Commonwealth, passed on the 27th day of May, 1867, hereby certify that the "Boston, Hartford and Erie Railroad Company" have in their judgment expended, since the passage of said Act, in work upon new road and equipment belonging to them, the sum of two hundred thousand dollars; and that this sum has been properly expended in the construction of new road and in the purchase of equipment.

Dated at Boston, this 31st day of July, A. D. 1868.

G. T. BIGELOW,
EMORY WASHBURN,
S. ASHBURNER,
    Commissioners.

[B.]

Commonwealth of Massachusetts.

Attorney General's Office,
Boston, 30 Court Street, August 21, 1868.

To His Excellency the Governor:

Sir:—I have your letter asking me to report fully in writing to you, and as early as may well be, upon the various matters which, by the act of 1867, are to be made to appear to the satisfaction of the governor and council and attorney general, before granting the first instalment of the state loan to the Boston, Hartford and Erie Railroad Company; and in reference thereto I beg leave respectfully to submit the following suggestions:

No evidence as to these matters has been laid before me from any source, except the report of the commissioners.

1. The Berdell mortgage appears to have been duly executed; but it does not appear that it has been duly recorded.

2. The official return of this company to the Commonwealth, published in January, 1866, shows that there were then nine existing mortgages covering some portions of their roads. The commissioners' report, if I understand it correctly, includes but eight. It does not appear whether or not any of the mortgages have been cancelled or discharged of record. Certainly some of them have not been; and it therefore remains to be shown that the mortgage debts secured by these underlying mortgages (and others, if there are others,) have been reduced to less than $1,000,000.

The mode most satisfactory to me of showing this would be as follows: *First,* to ascertain in detail all the mortgages that have ever been made, covering any part of the roads; the amount of bonds issued under each mortgage and secured thereby; whether any other debt or obligation or duty involving an expenditure of money is secured thereby; what amount of bonds secured by each mortgage has been taken up; what amount now remains outstanding; and what amount of interest is due on such as remain outstanding. *Then*, if the ·bonds or other debts or duties secured by any mortgage have all been taken up, to have a discharge of every such mortgage duly entered of record. *Finally*, if the bonds or other debts secured by any mortgage have been only partially taken up, to have a discharge *pro tanto* of every such mortgage duly entered of record; that is, a discharge as to all such bonds or debts as have been taken up; so that the security will only stand upon record as applicable to the outstanding bonds, debts or other duties.

It may be that this course is impracticable, as to entering a a discharge *pro tanto* of record. In that case, it seems to me that the evidence should be precise, to show the number of bonds or other debts that have been taken up or satisfied, and that the same have been cancelled.

At present, I am unable, from any facts within my knowledge, to make up such a statement in detail as to the number of mortgages that have been made, or the bonds or other debts or duties secured thereby, or the amount of bonds taken up, or the precise amount still outstanding and secured by each mortgage, or the interest remaining due thereon. It does not appear that any of the bonds have been cancelled which have been taken up.

3. The commissioners certify that they are satisfied that the railroad company have properly expended $200,000 in the construction of new road and purchase of equipment, since the act of 1867 was passed. This certificate would be entirely satisfactory to me if by the true construction of the statute I deemed myself at liberty to accept their judgment, without knowing the facts upon which it is founded. But in my opinion it was the intention of the legislature that there should be an independent judgment of the governor and council and attorney general, founded upon a knowledge of the facts.

I have the honor to be,
Very respectfully, your obedient servant,

CHARLES ALLEN.

4

[C.]

COMMONWEALTH OF MASSACHUSETTS.

COUNCIL CHAMBER, BOSTON, September, 1868.

The Committee of the Council, to whom was referred the report of the commissioners appointed with reference to the loan to the Boston, Hartford and Erie Railroad Company, together with the report of the attorney general thereon, have considered the same, and herewith submit their Report :—

The requirements of the Act of the year 1867, chapter 284, to be complied with on the part of said company, to entitle them to the first instalment of scrip or certificates of indebtedness, which compliance must be made to appear to the satisfaction of the governor and council and the attorney general, as also, in some particulars, to the commissioners, are as follows :—

1. The due execution of the mortgage to Berdell and others, trustees.

2. The proper registry of said mortgage.

3. The discharge of all underlying mortgages upon the franchise and property of said company, lying between the foot of Summer Street, in Boston, and the towns of Southbridge, in Massachusetts, and Willimantic, in Connecticut; or, that the mortgage debt secured by the underlying mortgages on said railroad between the points aforesaid has been reduced to less than one million of dollars; and that a bond of said company, satisfactory to the governor and council, shall be deposited with the treasurer of the Commonwealth, conditioned that the franchise and property of the company between the points aforesaid shall be protected from all uncancelled bonds secured by the underlying mortgages aforesaid.

4. That the company has properly expended two hundred thousand dollars in construction of new road and in the purchase of equipment. •

5. An agreement of the company, in form approved by the attorney general, and delivered to the treasurer of the Commonwealth, conditioned that said company shall comply with the provisions of said Act, and indemnify and save harmless the Commonwealth, from all expenses incurred, or loss or damage on account of said scrip, and that said company shall and will well and truly pay the principal and interest of said scrip when the same shall become due and payable, and deliver as security for the performance of the conditions of said agreement $133,333.33$\frac{1}{3}$, in the bonds secured by the said Berdell mortgage, to and for every one hundred thousand dollars in scrip to be issued to the company.

6. No scrip to be issued unless it shall be made to appear, to the satisfaction of the governor and council and commissioners, that the company will be able, either alone or with the aid of other parties than this Commonwealth, to complete a line of railway from Boston to Fishkill, within five years from the passage of the Act.

The Committee proceed to consider said requirements, in the order named, and to inquire as to the performance of these conditions on the part of the company, and their probable ability to complete the work.

1. It appears by the reports, both of the commissioners and the attorney general, that the Berdell mortgage has been duly executed.

2. We find, by a certificate made to us by the chairman of the commissioners, that said Berdell mortgage has been duly recorded.

3. We find it impracticable to require the cancellation and discharge of record of the underlying mortgages, inasmuch as there appears on all of them, with a single exception, to wit, that made by the South Midland Railroad Company, to be more or less outstanding bonds, as will more fully appear hereinafter. We therefore proceed to consider the alternative provision of the statute.

And, *first*, as to the outstanding bonds secured by the underlying mortgages ; and here the Committee seem to be compelled, in a great measure, to rely upon the report of the commissioners, who appear to have proceeded in the only practicable mode to ascertain the facts, viz.: by obtaining certificates or depositions from the proper officers in the several registries of deeds and other places, in the several States where the property of the company is situated, stating the number and terms of all mortgages made by the respective corporations which have been united with and merged into the Boston, Hartford and Erie Railroad Company, and by the sworn statements of one or more of the trustees named in the respective mortgages, and also the sworn statements of the treasurer of said company.

From these sources it appears that the mortgages and the bonds issued under the same upon the security of the road from Boston to Fishkill, and exclusive of those issued by the Hartford, Providence and Fishkill Company, are as follows:—

Boston and New York Central Railroad Co., .	$794,000 00
South Midland Railroad Co., ...	801,000 00
New York and Boston Railroad Co., upon one mortgage, ...	345,600 00
New York and Boston Railroad Co., upon another mortgage, ...	1,287,700 00
Charles River Railroad Co., ...	37,000 00
Norfolk County Railroad Company, .. .	414,350 00
Boston, Hartford and Erie Railroad Co., 1864,	4,500,000 00
Total, ...	$7,679,650 00

This is the amount of bonds issued upon what are called the underlying mortgages, and is exclusive of the indebtedness of the Providence, Hartford and Fishkill Railroad Company, which is not included in the direct line from Boston to Fishkill. The attorney general, in his report, calls attention to the report of the company made to the State in 1866, in which the number of mortgages is stated to be *nine*, and that the commissioners speak only of *eight*. This is explained by the fact that there were two mortgages made by the Hartford, Providence and Fishkill Company, both together amounting to $2,055,000, as stated by the commissioners, though treated by them as one mortgage.

There is a discrepancy of a few thousand dollars between the amount of issued bonds, as stated by the commissioners, and the statement of the treasurer of the company. This difference is explained by the commissioners thus: When they found variations in the testimony of the witnesses as to the amount of bonds issued, which did occur in a single instance, they, by way of precaution, adopted the larger sum or amount.

Of these bonds, it appears by the statement of William Dehon, Esq., who was employed by the commissioners to count the same, that the following bonds have been taken up by the Boston, Hartford and Erie Railroad Company, and are now held by them ready to be cancelled, viz.:—

South Midland Railroad Co., bonds, . .	$301,000 00
Norfolk County Railroad bonds, . . .	410,750 00
Boston and New York Central bonds, . .	760,000 00
New York and Boston Railroad Co. bonds, .	885,900 00
do. do. notes, .	277,000 00
Charles River Railroad Co. bonds, . . .	16,000 00
Boston, Hartford and Erie Railroad Co. notes,	4,022,000 00
Total, ...	$6,672,650 00

In addition to the bonds and notes counted by Mr. Dehon, it appears, by the sworn statement of Mr. Barry, assistant treasurer, furnished to the Committee, and also by the evidence of Mr. Farwell, one of the directors of the company, that $426,100 of the bonds of the New York and Boston Railroad Company were never actually disposed of by the company, and are now in the custody of its treasurer, but were not counted by Mr. Dehon, though they were included by the commissioners as a part of the mortgaged indebtedness of the company. It appears, therefore, that these bonds should have been counted by Mr. Dehon.

It further appears that since the count by Mr. Dehon the company has retired the additional amount of $47,900 of the outstanding bonds. Add these amounts to the bonds counted by Mr. Dehon and we have an aggregate of $7,146,650, thus leaving outstanding at this date bonds to the amount of only $533,000. The company believe the amount to be considerably less. The committee are satisfied from the evidence that the company has reduced the said indebtedness to less than $1,000,000. -

The question of the bond to be given by the company next claims our attention. The second section of the statute provides that in the event that the underlying mortgages are not cancelled and discharged, a bond of the company, satisfactory to the governor and council, conditioned that the franchise and property of the company, named and described in the Berdell mortgage, lying between certain points named in the Act, shall be protected from all such uncancelled bonds. What bond ought the governor and council to require? The Committee are of opinion that a bond with sufficient sureties, satisfactory to the governor and council, in form such as the attorney general shall approve, in the penal sum of one million dollars, should be made and executed by the company and deposited with the treasurer of the Commonwealth.

Before the issue of any scrip by the Commonwealth the bonds and notes aforesaid should be counted and cancelled, or otherwise stamped in such manner, satisfactory to the attorney general, as shall clearly indicate that they are not further negotiable, and certificates thereof made by the commissioners or under their direction, furnished to and deposited with the treasurer of the Commonwealth.

4. We are abundantly satisfied by the evidence produced before us that the company has properly expended two hundred thousand dollars in the construction of new road and in the purchase of equipment, since the date of the passage of the Act.

5. It is unnecessary for the Committee to repeat the requirements under the fifth head, as they relate solely to acts hereafter to be performed to entitle the company to receive the scrip.

6. Will the company be able, either alone or with the aid of other parties than this Commonwealth, to complete a line of railway from Boston to Fishkill within five years from the passage of the Act? Of the 226 miles from Boston to Fishkill, there are now in operation 123.43 miles. The parts not in operation consist, *first*, of the line from Mechanicsville to Willimantic, 26.28 miles. This portion is under contract with a responsible party, and the work, we understand, is progressing satisfactorily, and will probably be completed in October, 1869. *Second*, the line from Waterbury to Fishkill, 76.39 miles. This

line is also under contract, and work thereon has been commenced. Mr. Ashburner expresses to the Committee his confident opinion that the time allowed by law for the completion of the road to Fishkill is ample. From the careful estimate made up in detail by Mr. Ashburner, and furnished to the Committee, we find that the unfinished sections of the road can be completed, with a moderate equipment, at a cost not to exceed $8,850,000. Of this sum, something more than $500,000 has already been paid by the company; so that the sum required. for the completion of the line may be stated, as an outside estimate, at the sum of $8,350,000.

The floating debt of the company is stated to be, exclusive of certain disputed claims, mentioned in the commissioners' report, $1,022,988.31, and interest notes given in exchange of mortgage bonds, $1,127,744.14, which are payable in 1872 without interest.

The available means of the company, upon which they rely to enable them to complete their road, may be stated briefly thus :—

Cash in bank, ... - .	$2,000,000 00
Acceptances of Erie Railroad Company,. . .	1,574,000 00
Berdell mortgage bonds, after deducting $4,000,000 for deposit with the State, and $533,000 for the redemption of outstanding bonds, estimated at 80 per cent., . .	3,632,000 00
50,0000 shares of capital stock, at $20, . ..	1,000,000 00
If, to these amounts, we add the State loan, which, if granted, will be available from time to time as the work progresses, . .	3,000,000 00
We have, ...	$11,206,000 00

In addition to this, the company has its road and rolling-stock, including the Hartford, Providence and Fishkill Railroad, above its mortgages, the value of which the commissioners estimate at not less than twelve millions of dollars.

With these means, present and prospective, at the disposal of the company, without further statement of details, the Committee cannot reasonably doubt their ability and determination to complete a line of railway from Boston to Fishkill within the time limited by the Act of the legislature.

The apparent interest of the company, also, to secure a speedy completion of the road, to enable their stock and bond-holders to reap the benefit of their investments, must form a powerful inducement to its officers to bend all their energies to the successful completion of the work.

The Committee, therefore, recommend the issue of the first instalment of one hundred thousand dollars to the Boston, Hartford and Erie Railroad Company, upon the performance of the further conditions required by the aforesaid Act, in the manner herein before indicated.

THOS. TALBOT.
CHAS. ENDICOTT.
PETER HARVEY.
H. G. KNIGHT.
R. G. USHER.

[D.]

COMMONWEALTH OF MASSACHUSETTS.

EXECUTIVE DEPARTMENT, }
BOSTON, September 12, 1868. }

To the Honorable Messrs. GEORGE T. BIGELOW and EMORY WASHBURN, and SAMUEL ASHBURNER, Esquire, *Commissioners, &c., &c.*:

GENTLEMEN:—Your report upon the matters involved in the question of granting the loan of three million dollars to the Boston, Hartford and Erie Railroad Company was referred by me on its receipt to a committee of the Council. This committee has prosecuted further inquiries upon the whole subject, and has now submitted its report.

Their original report is herewith forwarded to you for your perusal, and as I do not wish to delay this question by making a copy I will thank you to return the same to me, together with the communication of the Attorney General which is also herewith transmitted to you.

In endeavoring to satisfy myself whether the Boston, Hartford and Erie Railroad Company will be able, either alone, or with the aid of other parties than the Commonwealth of Massachusetts, to complete a line of railway from Boston to Fishkill within five years from the date of the passage of the Act of the legislature (May 27, 1867,) I desire to avail myself of the provision of the sixth section of the Act, and ask from you advice and information somewhat more in detail than heretofore given, in respect to the disbursements necessary to be made by the company, and their resources.

From the statement of Mr. Ashburner to the committee of the council, it appears that his estimate of the sum to be allowed for the completion of the line of railway, with a moderate equipment, is $8,850,000 00

To this sum it would appear that the following
sums should be added, as existing debts of the
company, irrespective of the Berdell bonds, and
the other outstanding bonds :—

Floating debt, ...	$1,022,988	00
Interest notes, ...	1,127,744	00
Certain other debts, in round numbers, . .	75,000	00
	$11,075,732	00

In order to ascertain whether the above sum of $11,075,732
correctly represents the approximate aggregate sum that the
company will be called upon to meet, as liabilities, before the
probable completion of their line of railway, will you inform
me :

1. Whether for any reason now existing any deduction
should be made from the above named sum ?

2. Whether the commissioners have so far investigated the
other claims, referred to in their report, which have been presented or are held against the company, described as "sundry
indefinite claims for land" and "a claim made for certain
alleged preferred stock in the Hartford, Providence and Fishkill Railroad" as to be satisfied that they are in law invalid,
and that the company will not have to pay out any considerable
sum in contesting or compromising the same ; and the approximate amount of these claims, as made against the company ?

3. Whether the relations existing between the Boston, Hartford and Erie Railroad Company, and the Hartford, Providence and Fishkill Company, will involve the payment of any
sum by the former company, except the bonds secured by mortgage upon the road of the latter company, amounting, for principal, to $2,055,000, and for interest to $170,000 ?

4. Whether under any existing contracts, or in order to
carry out any other work or plan now projected, not embraced in the completion of the direct line from Boston to
Fishkill, the Boston, Hartford and Erie Railroad Company will
be called on to pay out any sums of money ? as, for instance,
in prosecuting work upon a railroad to New Haven, or upon
any other branch road ?

5. Whether or not additions should be made to the other
sums above referred to, for interest money, and if so, how

much ? Is it the case that upon the Berdell bonds already given out, interest is now running upon $5,000,000, and that interest will be due upon the remaining $5,963,000 in July, 1870, and semi-annually thereafter ; that interest will be due upon the interest notes given upon the exchange of bonds, to the amount of $1,127,744, on January 1st, 1870, and regularly thereafter ; and that interest is now running upon the floating debt of $1,022,988 ? Should not interest be added for the amount of bonds which may be issued by the State ? And are there any other items which ought to be taken into account in this connection, and what sum, in all, would it be proper to include, as probably necessary to be paid for interest, before the completion of the work ? Has any portion of the Berdell bonds been issued in sterling currency, and if so how much, and is the interest thereon payable in coin ?

6. Is it probable that the remaining original bonds now outstanding and secured by mortgage can be exchanged for Berdell bonds ?

The resources of the company, which are relied upon to enable them to complete the railroad, so far as made known to me, appear to be the following :—

Cash, and acceptances of the Erie R. R., .	$3,574,000 00
Amount expected from the State, . .	3,000,000 00
Berdell bonds remaining after all necessary appropriations of them, ...	
50,000 shares of stock of the company yet unissued, ...	
Add amount already paid towards the construction of the work, as appears by the report of Mr. Ashburner to the committee of the council, and which, therefore, should be deducted from his estimate of $8,850,000, .	500,000 00

In reference to the resources of the company, will you inform me—

1. Whether any items which can be reckoned in money, other than those above named, should, in your opinion, be taken into the account in estimating their ability to complete the work ; and, if so, what they are ?

2. Whether the cash, stated at $2,000,000, is now actually on hand, and at the present absolute disposal of the company; and whether the acceptances, stated at $1,574,000, are absolute, or dependent upon any condition; and whether there is anything to prevent the money from being realized on them at once? I think it my duty to require the best evidence upon these points. I desire that the commissioners should have personal inspection of the acceptances, and give me their opinion whether payment of them can be enforced under the laws of New York.

3. What amount of the Berdell bonds will the company have available to be disposed of after making all necessary appropriations of them? At present, they appear to have sold or exchanged, ... $10,963,000 00

This leaves a balance of, ... $9,037,000 00
There are required for the State, . . . 4,000,000 00

Balance, ... $5,037,000 00

There appears to be a balance of other mortgage bonds now outstanding of $2,790,800, including those of the Providence, Hartford and Fishkill Railroad. Will not Berdell bonds to this amount be required under the terms of the mortgage, to be exchanged for all those other outstanding bonds? Or, if not so exchanged, should not the amount of those outstanding bonds be added to the liabilities of the company?

4. Whether, in your opinion, it is safe to assume that the balance of the bonds and the 50,000 shares of stock can and will be disposed of by the company at the present market rates?

5. I will also thank you to mention any other consideration that may occur to you as bearing upon the question, whether or not the resources of the company are sufficient to enable them to meet the disbursements required for the completion of the railroad as contemplated by the statute.

I remain, with great respect,
Your obedient servant,

ALEX. H. BULLOCK,
Governor.

Boston, September 21, 1868.

His Excellency A. H. Bullock, *Governor, &c.*:

Dear Sir :—The undersigned, Commissioners, &c., have the honor to acknowledge the receipt of your Excellency's communication of the 12th instant, and hasten to reply to the several inquiries thereby propounded to them.

In doing so, they return, as desired, your Excellency's communication, together with the report of a committee of the council, and the opinion of the attorney general upon the subject of a loan to the Boston, Hartford and Erie Railroad Company.

To your Excellency's first and second inquiry, they answer,—

1. That from the floating debt, $1,022,988, there should be deducted $418,553.46, the same having been paid since their former report, by applying a part of th $2,000,000 then on deposit for that purpose, as per annexed certificate of Mr. Barry.

2. That the item of interest notes, $1,127,744, has no connection with the present ability of the company to complete said road, because they do not, in the judgment of the commissioners, form any lien on the same. They do not carry interest until January 1, 1870, and are not due and payable until September 1, 1872, which is subsequent to the time when, by the Act, the road is to be completed to the Hudson River.

3. In respect to the item of $75,000 for " certain other debts, &c.," the Commissioners have submitted the same to the inspection of Thomas E. Graves, the legal counsel and adviser of said company, and required of him to state, upon oath, what parts of said claims are, in his judgment and belief, due and collectable against the company. He has done so, and his closing statement is in these words : " These include all claims presented the honorable commissioners, and by them handed to me. My judgment and belief is, that there is not over six thousand dollars of the whole claims can or will ever be col-

lected out of the Boston, Hartford and Erie Railroad Company, or from any estate in its possession."

The Commissioners have no other means of forming an opinion of the amount due and collectible of said supposed claims. Nor are they advised whether this indebtedness would affect the ability of the company to complete their road any otherwise than the fact of owing that amount of money would be likely to do.

In reply to your Excellency's third inquiry, the Commissioners would state that they applied to Messrs. George M. Bartholomew and Calvin Day, who, they are advised, hold the Hartford, Providence and Fishkill Railroad as trustees under mortgages thereon, and are informed by them, by letter bearing date September 18, 1868, as follows: "There are not, within my knowledge, any obligations of the first named company, (Boston, Hartford and Erie Railroad Company,) except such as are recorded in the contract between the two companies, dated August 28, 1863, and such as would follow the purchase of any property, i. e., that it is liable for the existing mortgage. I refer to the $2,055,000 Hartford, Providence and Fishkill Railroad bonds." From this, and a similar oral statement made by one or more of the officers of the Boston, Hartford and Erie Railroad Company, the Commissioners are of opinion that the relations existing between the Boston, Hartford and Erie Railroad Company and the Hartford, Providence and Fishkill Railroad Company, will not involve the payment of any sum by the former company except the bonds and interest referred to in said inquiry.

We have ascertained by inquiry from the trustees aforesaid, that all liabilities under the contract above named are secured by stock placed in the hands of said trustees, in pursuance of the provisions of the contract above named.

To the fourth inquiry of your Excellency, the Commissioners state that they have inquired if any contracts, such as are referred to in said inquiry, are in existence, under which the Boston, Hartford and Erie Railroad Company will be called upon to pay out any sums of money, and are satisfied that none such exist upon which said company are legally liable, or which can be enforced against them before they shall have completed their road to Fishkill. They have, among other things, referred to a contract between the New York and Boston Railroad Company and the Boston, Hartford and Erie Railroad Company, dated December 16, 1864, in reference to a railroad to New Haven, which, as it seems to the Commissioners, in effect refers the ultimate construction of said road to the voluntary action of the Boston, Hartford and Erie Railroad Company.

To your Excellency's fifth interrogatory, the Commissioners state that they called upon Mr. Barry, the assistant-treasurer of the Boston, Hartford and Erie Railroad, to answer upon oath as to the facts inquired of therein. In answer thereto, he stated " that the company has sold five millions of dollars of bonds under the Berdell mortgage, on which interest will fall due January, 1869, and paid out ninety thousand of said bonds on account of bonds purchased, on which also interest will fall due in January, 1869. No other of said bonds, with coupons attached, and due before July, 1870, are sold or issued." He then states that the floating debt had been reduced, as is above stated, and adds : " On this last amount ($609,190.54,) interest is payable at various times on the items of the amount, but in most cases payable as the sums making the amount fall due. The notes given for interest on exchange of bonds fall due 1872, and interest on them, July, 1870, that being six months' interest from January, 1870. There is no interest due on any bond debts of the company, so far as I know or believe, except what is overdue on the bonds which have not been taken up or exchanged, the principal sum being about $450,000, and interest overdue about $50,000, which amount it is expected will be arranged by exchange of bonds."

The Commissioners have no reason to doubt the correctness of the above statement, and give it as the answer to said inquiry in respect to interest. Both the assistant treasurer, Mr. Barry, and J. C. Bancroft Davis, one of the trustees in the Berdell mortgage bonds, state, in writing to the Commissioners, that none of said bonds have been issued in sterling currency, and such the Commissioners believe to be the case.

To the sixth interrogatory of your Excellency, the Commissioners say that if the proposed loan should be made by the Commonwealth to the Boston, Hartford and Erie Railroad

Company, they have no doubt whatever that the remaining original bonds can be exchanged for Berdell bonds. More than sixty thousand dollars of such bonds have been taken up and exchanged since Mr. Dehon counted the bonds of the company, which, by his certificate, was July 25, 1868, and if this is done the interest upon these now outstanding bonds, as the Commissioners understand, will be suspended and postponed to 1870 and 1890, to swell the item of "interest notes."

In reply to your Excellency's first inquiry on page 9 of your communication to the Commissioners, they would state that it appears by the deposition of G. M. Bartholomew, that there was in the hands of the treasurer of the City of Hartford, January 1, 1868, the sum of $109,835.22, belonging to the Hartford, Providence and Fishkill road, and held in trust as a sinking fund to be applied in payment of the mortgage bonds outstanding against said road. And that another sum for the same purpose was in the hands of the treasurer of the City of Providence, reported to be in May, 1866, $71,888.40.

By a printed and published statement made by the Hartford, Providence and Fishkill Railroad Company, purporting to bear date March 16, 1868, these sinking funds are stated to be $109,835.22 and $83,619.18. These two sums, $193,454.40, should be taken as cash assets of the company so far at least as to be offset against the item of interest due on the mortgage bonds of $2,055,500, stated as being $170,000, in your Excellency's third inquiry above replied to.

To the second interrogatory of your Excellency, so far as it relates to the certificate of deposit for $2,000,000, the Commissioners are entirely satisfied that when their former Report was made that sum was *bona fide* on deposit belonging to said company. They are satisfied further that since that time a part of the sum has been used or loaned on interest, with satisfactory security, and that the annexed statement of Mr. Barry, as to its condition and disposal, is true.

So far as said interrogatory relates to the acceptances of the Erie Railroad for "$1,570,400," the Commissioners understand and believe the facts to be as follows:—

The Erie Railroad purchased of the Boston, Hartford and Erie Railroad Berdell mortgage bonds to the amount of $5,000,000, agreeing to give therefor $4,000,000. Of this, they paid the sum of $2,000,000, which was the money above mentioned as having been put on deposit, and gave their acceptances for the sum of $1,570,400. They have seen the original and annex a copy of one of them, and so far as form and consideration is concerned everything appears to be, and in their judgment is, correct. On the 8th day of October, 1867, the Erie Railroad Company agreed with the Boston, Hartford and Erie Railroad, in writing, a copy of which is in the Commissioners' hands, to guaranty the payment of the interest upon $4,000,000 of the bonds, secured by the Berdell mortgage, to the holders thereof, which guaranty was to be in these words, " In consideration of the provisions of a contract of even date for the use of the Boston, Hartford and Erie Railroad by the Erie Railway Company, the Erie Railway Company hereby agrees with the holder of this bond that the several interest warrants hereto attached shall be paid as they respectively mature. Witness the seal of the Erie Railway Company and the signature of its secretary of the City of New York, the 8th day of October, A. D. 1867."

The Commissioners are in possession of an original opinion, in writing, given by D. B. Eaton and William M. Evarts, Esquires, of New York, dated July 30, 1868, that the contract of the 8th of October, 1867, whereby the Erie Railway Company " agreed to be responsible for the payment of interest on bonds of the Boston, Hartford and Erie Railroad Company are legal and valid provisions, and that such bonds bearing the indorsement of the Erie Railway Company for the payment of interest made pursuant to said contract, are binding on that company according to the purport of said contract and endorsement."

It would appear from this opinion that the Erie Railway Company are authorized by the laws of New York to enter into contracts to aid the Boston, Hartford and Erie Railroad Company in constructing their road. The acceptances above referred to were made and executed for this purpose, and if the guaranty of the interest on the bonds was a valid contract under the laws of New York, we see no reason why the acceptances are not also valid.

In further answer, the Commissioners have the statement under oath of Mr. Barry, the Assistant Treasurer, as aforesaid,

C

that he knows nothing why the said acceptances are not absolutely and *bona fide* due and payable, or why they will not be paid at maturity. The same information is given them by the president and other officers of the company; and the Commissioners are fully satisfied that the same are held in good faith by the Boston, Hartford and Erie Railroad Company for a valuable consideration, and with the confidence that they can and will be duly paid according to their tenor.

The Commissioners do not undertake to express an opinion upon the liability of the acceptors as a matter of local law, and refer, therefore, to the opinions of the distinguished gentlemen above mentioned upon that point. But if, as they are informed and believe, the Erie Railway Company have received and made use of as their own, five millions of the Berdell mortgage bonds, and have accepted bills drawn on that company for $1,570,400, in part payment of the same, the Commissioners cannot doubt that the Erie Railway Company are liable therefor, either as acceptors or for the value of the bonds so purchased, received and used by them.

In answer to the third interrogatory on page 10, the Commissioners state, as follows:—

They understand, as implied in said interrogatory, that of the Berdell bonds there have been sold or disposed of $10,963,000.

They understand that it will require the amount of $2,588,500 to cancel and retire the outstanding bonds secured by mortgages upon the Hartford, Providence and Fishkill Railroad, and upon other parts of the road of the Boston, Hartford and Erie Railroad Company.

If to this is added the bonds proposed to be taken by the State, $4,000,000, it will have for the immediate use of the company, a balance in bonds of $2,448,500.

In this the Commissioners assume, that so many of the Berdell bonds as will be necessary to retire and cancel all outstanding bonds which form a lien upon any part of the road or franchise of the company, are to be treated as if applied to that purpose. But they do not include the $170,000 of interest in arrear, for the reasons above stated, and they assume the balance due on the bonds other than those of the Hartford,

Providence and Fishkill road, at the sum stated by the Council, $533,000.

In answer to the fourth interrogatory of your Excellency, the Commissioners have no doubt that if the loan of the State shall be made as proposed, the balance of the Berdell bonds could be at once sold for cash in the market as high as the present market value; and their belief is, that the price would in that event rise considerably above the present market value.

And as for the 50,000 shares of stock, responsible gentlemen have offered, in writing, and the same is now in the Commissioners' hands, to give and pay $1,000,000 for said 50,000 shares, and the Commissioners believe this offer to be *bona fide* made.

In reply to your Excellency's last and general inquiry, the Commissioners would respectfully present their views by the following exhibit, which they believe is justified and sustained by the facts already in possession of your Excellency.

Taking Mr. Ashburner's original calculations for construction and equipping the road, ...	$8,850,000 00
Add to this the balance of the floating debt, .	604,434 00
It makes an aggregate, ...	$9,454,434 00

The assets or means of the Company already paid towards construction, as stated by the report of the Council,	$500,000 00
Acceptances of Erie road, ...	1,570,400 00
Loan of the Commonwealth, ...	3,000,000 00
Seventy per cent. on balance of Berdell bonds,	1,713,950 00
Cash on hand on deposit, ...	824,427 00
" on call loan, ...	530,511 00
	$8,139,288 00

By the returns of the doings of the roads the last year, the net earnings of the Hartford, Providence and Fishkill were $142,688.62, and those of the other parts exceeded the cost of running the same and repairs, so that it would seem a fair estimate to offset the accruing interest against the earnings of roads.

There will then be left to be provided for over and above the assumed cash assets of the company,.   .   . $1,315,146 00.

This amount of floating debt, which is all that would be outstanding at the completion of the road, due from a company which had expended the foregoing amount in the construction of its road, with no other large liabilities maturing before July, 1872, would not materially impair or affect their ability to complete the road by the time required by the Act. But it is also to be borne in mind, that the company is in possession of stock which is alleged to be of the value of $1,000,000, and that, in the above estimate, the bonds of the company available to them are estimated at seventy per cent. only.

And in view of what now appears to them from the foregoing facts and the apparently prosperous condition of the enterprise, the Commissioners· respectfully report their confidence and belief that the company have the ability to complete the road within the time prescribed by the Act, if the work should be carried on with energy, and the funds and resources of the company are prudently and honestly appropriated and applied.

> GEO. TYLER BIGELOW,
> EMORY WASHBURN,
> S. ASHBURNER,
> *Commissioners.*

BOSTON, HARTFORD AND ERIE RAILROAD CO.,
OFFICE OF THE TREASURER, BOSTON, Sept. 16, 1868.

Memorandum of $2,000,000 held by Boston, Hartford and Erie Railroad Company.

Paid on account Floating Debt, . . .	$418,553 46
" N. C. Munson, on account, . . .	226,507 38
Memorandum of A. G. Farwell & Co., . .	580,511 40
On hand in Bank of Commerce, . . .	824,427 76
Total, ...	$2,000,000 00

H. S. BARRY, *A. Treas.*

[E.]

COMMONWEALTH OF MASSACHUSETTS.

EXECUTIVE DEPARTMENT,
BOSTON, September 24, 1868.

To the Directors of the Boston, Hartford and Erie Railroad Company :

GENTLEMEN :—I invite your attention to a few questions which have not been answered to my entire satisfaction, and which, to avoid delay, I propound directly to you. I inclose copies of the communications which have been made to me by commissioners, since they are referred to in this communication.

1. In their first report, the commissioners allowed about $70,000 for certain claims presented to them, besides referring to certain other claims, mentioned on page 5 of my communication to them. In their present report, the $70,000 is reduced to $6,000 on the statement of Mr. Graves ; and the other claims are not adverted to.

2. As to the relations of the Boston, Hartford and Erie Company to the Providence and Fishkill : A contract is referred to, which has not been produced. On what terms can the former company get possession of the latter company's road ?

3. Upon the interest question : assuming that the road will be finished in May, 1872, there appear to be the following sums for interest, due before that time :—

Two years' interest on the interest notes of $1,127,744, that is, interest falling due July, 1870, January and July, 1871 and January, 1872, at seven per cent., ... $157,884 00

Three and a half years' interest—that is from January, 1869, to January, 1872, including both dates—on $5,090,000 Berdell bonds, as by letter of commissioners, at seven per cent., 1,247,050 00

Interest on $6,000,000 Berdell bonds additional, now sold or exchanged, July, 1870, and thereafter two years, at seven per cent.,   .   . 840,000 00

Interest on $5,000,000 Berdell bonds left remaining, of which $2,600,000 in round numbers will be used to retire the rest of the outstanding bonds, and $2,400,000 will be sold—two years' interest being that falling due July, 1870 and thereafter, ... $700,000 00

Interest now overdue on outstanding bonds, as by commissioners' letter, ... 50,000 00

—————————

$2,994,934 00

Interest on floating debt—balance $609,000 (depending on when it becomes due.)

Interest on State scrip, from time when it is issued.

The commissioners report that the probable earnings may be assumed as sufficient to take care of the interest.

4. It is said that the Erie Railroad bought $5,000,000 of Berdell bonds for $4,000,000, paying $2,000,000 in money, and $1,570,400 in acceptances.

$2,000,000 00		$4,000,000 00
1,570,400 00		3,570,400 00
—————————		—————————
$3,570,400 00	.	$429,600 00

In what manner do they receive payment for the balance ?

5. Law question as to acceptances.

" The Erie Railroad Company, for the purpose of aiding the Boston, Hartford and Erie Railroad Company in the construction of their railroad, having bought of the latter company their mortgage bonds to the amount of $5,000,000, and received the same, agreeing to pay for the same the sum of $4,000,000, and having paid therefor partly in money and partly by giving their acceptances payable at various dates hereafter ; the question is, whether said acceptances are legally binding upon the Erie Railroad Company, and whether individual stockholders of that company can legally prevent the payment thereof by injunction or otherwise, and whether or not there was anything in the action of the legislature of New York of last winter affecting this subject."

ALEXANDER H. BULLOCK.

Boston, September 26, 1868.

To His Excellency Hon. A. H. Bullock:—

Dear Sir,—Your favor of the 24th inst. was duly received, and in reply, we have the honor to submit the following answers to your interrogatories.

Very respectfully yours,

JOHN S. ELDREDGE.
HENRY N. FARWELL.
JAMES S. WHITNEY.
J. W. CONVERSE.

1. In answer to question No. 1 of His Excellency, (of this date,) the Boston, Hartford and Erie Railroad Company answer: That the commissioners published notices, asking for all claims to be shown, which any had against the franchises or estates which the Boston, Hartford and Erie Railroad Company held, and the claims brought in were submitted to this company. Between the time of the first and second report, sundry of them were taken up, and on the day of the statement of Mr. Graves, the amount of the claims presented were believed to be only valid to less than six thousand dollars. The commissioners have the original claims.

2. The contract with the Hartford, Providence and Fishkill Railroad Company, referred to, was furnished the honorable commissioners. It was in reference to the purchase and sale of said Hartford, Providence and Fishkill Railroad to the Boston, Hartford and Erie Railroad Company. The purchase was made under special power from legislatures of Rhode Island and Connecticut, and the conveyance was by deed. There is no provisions as to having possession of the road, other than found in the mortgage deeds. These provide that whenever all overdue debt and interest secured under the mortgages

are paid, the road, &c., shall be given to its owner, i. e., the Boston, Hartford and Erie Railroad Company. Of the bonds secured, one million is due in 1876. The balance is overdue on the face of bonds, but the trustees advise us they have, with contract with holders of the overdue bonds, attached new coupons, to fall due semi-annually, until 1876, and that thus the payment of the principal is extended until that time. But at the most, on payment of one million of dollars, and back interest of less than one hundred and fifty thousand dollars, possession can be had at once. There is a sinking fund against the above bonds, of about two hundred thousand dollars.

3. Upon the interest question : (1.) The written contracts for construction of our road from Boston to the Hudson River provide for the completion of the whole line before 1870 ; and so the item for interest to accrue on the interest notes to fall due after January, 1870, it seems to us, should not stand as a charge against our ability to complete the road. (2.) The interest on the $5,000,000 Berdell bonds must be paid from earnings, or bonds or notes. This will be a year's interest on them before completion of the road. (3.) Interest on $6,000,000 not sold, reckoned at $840,000, after 1870, we consider should not now enter into the account. (3½.) Interest on $5,000,000, left remaining, we consider not to be accounted, for we do not expect to sell them until the cash on hand and the State aid is exhausted. (4.) Interest on $50,000, overdue interest on outstanding bonds. Our answer to this to commissioners was, and we repeat it here : The old bonds are being exchanged daily, and we expect all that amount, or most of it, will be absorbed in interest notes to fall due in 1872, and so not a charge on any present funds or bonds. (5.) Interest on floating debt we regard a proper present charge.

The income on our running roads today show us we can from that source pay the interest on all bonds out, and such as will be put out, including any State aid bonds, and that when our road is completed to Willimantic, which is contracted to be done within a year, that then the income will exceed any bonds or other indebtedness out. This is believed to be true, with no road completed beyond Waterbury. This, we understand, to be the opinion of the honorable commissioners.

4. The four hundred twenty-nine thousand six hundred dollars inquired about: Of this amount, three hundred and twenty-five thousand dollars ($325,000) is in hand and present available funds, cash, in possession of the president and vice-president, and the balance has been expended in the construction account of the railway.

5. Acceptances: The opinion of Mr. Evarts and others was had as to power of Erie Railway Company to contract with and indorse the bonds of this company, and since the question has been raised on the acceptances, we have sent for and obtained Mr. Evarts's opinion in the above matter. We take pleasure in handing herewith that opinion. Hope it will be found to give your Excellency the same confidence in our course, we feel ourselves.

7

NEW YORK, September 25, 1868.

MY DEAR SIR:—I understand that an opinion is desired from me upon the following question, arising upon the relations of the Erie Railway Company and the Boston, Hartford and Erie Railroad Company, in the transaction of the purchase of the bonds of the latter company by the Erie Railway Company.

The purchase of the bonds of the Boston, Hartford and Erie Company was made by the Erie Railway Company upon the advice of counsel that the transaction was within the competency of that company, and that consequently a contract for the purchase, in whole or in part executory, could be enforced against the Erie Railway Company. Upon this opinion the acceptances of the Erie Railway Company, still held by the Boston, Hartford and Erie Railroad Company, representing a portion of the price paid for the bonds, are understood to be valid and enforceable by law.

Now the question proposed to me is, what would be the legal position of the Boston, Hartford and Erie Company towards the Erie Railway Company in case, upon a refusal of the latter to pay these acceptances, their collection should be defeated at law, on the ground that the purchase of the bonds was *ultra vires*, and the acceptances of the company given therefor could not be enforced? I do not understand that this question is raised upon any interest or intent of the Erie Railway Company thus to avoid the payment of the acceptances, or in any doubt of the validity of the same on the part of the Boston, Hartford and Erie Company, but for the purpose of ascertaining what would be the rights of the two companies in case the direct collection of the acceptances should be successfully resisted.

I have given this question consideration, but have only an opportunity, at present, to state the conclusion to which I have come.

If the Erie Railway Company should avoid the payment of the acceptances outstanding in part payment of the contract price for the bonds purchased, on the ground that the contract was beyond the competency of the purchasing company, I am of opinion that the Boston, Hartford and Erie Company would be able to maintain an equitable action for the restoration of the bonds which formed the consideration of the contract thus repudiated, and, in so far as the Erie Railway Company should prove unable to make such restoration, for an account of the proceeds or value of the bonds sold or disposed of by the Erie Railway Company, I understand the law now to be well settled that a corporation repudiating a *contract* as *ultra vires* cannot retain the fruits of that contract as if it had acknowledged and performed it.

The practical consequence, then, in the actual case proposed to me, would be that the Boston, Hartford and Erie Company would be protected from loss upon the hypothesis that the outstanding acceptances should be held invalid upon the ground suggested.

I am, with great respect,
Yours, very truly,

WM. M. EVARTS.

Jno. S. Eldridge, Esq., *Pres't, &c., &c.*

Commonwealth of Massachusetts.
Executive Department.

Boston,

[F.]

COMMONWEALTH OF MASSACHUSETTS.

ATTORNEY GENERAL'S OFFICE, }
BOSTON, 30 COURT STREET, Oct. 1, 1868. }

SIR :—The opinion of Mr. Evarts, which you have inclosed
to me, although not in terms covering the element of the effect
of the action or non-action of the legislature of New York,
which was embraced in your question, yet may well be received
as a satisfactory answer to the question, and a solution of the
doubt as to the legal liability of the Erie Railroad Company
upon their contract, for the practical purposes of the present
inquiry.

I have the honor to be,
Very respectfully,
Your obedient servant,

CHARLES ALLEN.

HIS EXCELLENCY THE GOVERNOR.

[G.]

COMMONWEALTH OF MASSACHUSETTS.

ATTORNEY GENERAL'S OFFICE,
BOSTON, 30 COURT STREET, October 6, 1868.

SIR:—As, at the close of your own investigations into the matters involved in the application of the Boston, Hartford and Erie Railroad Company, it will be convenient for you to have my conclusions upon those questions in respect to which my concurrent action is required, I beg to say, having reference to my former report of August 21, in addition thereto, as follows:

I am now satisfied—

1. That the Berdell mortgage has been duly recorded.

2. That the mortgage debts secured by the underlying mortgages, referred to in section 2 of the Act, have been reduced to less than one million dollars, and so far below that sum that the bond recommended by the committee of the Council will render a more exact result unnecessary.

3. That the company has properly expended two hundred thousand dollars in construction of new road and in the purchase of equipment, as required in the same section.

I have the honor to be,
Very respectfully,
Your obedient servant,

CHARLES ALLEN.

HIS EXCELLENCY THE GOVERNOR.